Business Leaders Praise
Ten Tactics for Successful Family Companies:

"Every family business has its own unique dynamics, intricacies, and challenges. Craig does an outstanding job of addressing these difficult matters. He touches on issues that any family business owner is sure to experience and presents practical solutions for these situations to achieve lasting success."

Ron Kruszewski, Chairman & CEO, Stifel Financial Corp.
Investment Firm – *stifel.com*

"Enjoyed it! This handbook is a very concise and fundamental guide to improving any business, and particularly for the unique challenges associated with a family business."

John Tracy (G2), CEO, Dot Foods
USA's Largest Food Redistributor – *dotfoods.com*

"Considering the abundance of books out there, it's refreshing to find one as practical and concise as this. For any business, but especially family-owned, Craig's tips are essential to instill professionalism and achieve world class performance. A must read!"

Tom Phillips (G1), CEO & Founder, Weekends Only
Regional Furniture Outlet – *weekendsonly.com*

"Wonderful resource for all business managers! The family-owned company will especially benefit as it applies to the challenges faced by the management team and how to overcome them. Well done!"

Lynn Sansone (G2), President, GEM Transportation
Chauffeur Service – *gemtransportation.com*

"Being part of a family business for 30 years, I loved reading the wisdom of your Ten Tactics for Successful Family Companies. You are spot on and your tips will help family businesses large and small prosper. Now that is something to celebrate!"

Jim Forsyth (G2), CEO, Moto, Inc.
Regional Convenience Stores – *mymotomart.com*

"Good stuff! This is a concise, yet excellent work that really speaks to creating a sustainable family business. Following Palubiak's tips we have thrived during the most recent economic downturn. Much thanks!"

Mike O'Shea (G4), President, O'Shea Builders
Commercial Construction – *osheabuilders.com*

"This is a quick read full of useful advice for any manager. I especially liked the discussion on dealing with different personality styles within the family-owned business. Craig has a unique ability to simplify complex issues."

Evan Ballman (G2), President, Motor Appliance Corporation
Global Manufacturer – *macmc.com*

"This book embodies many things we have been working on for several years. Yet, starting with its title, I now realize how much of the family business remains hidden and not fully defined. Craig, thanks for the continuing push!"

Randy Hilleren (G1), President, FastDirect Communications
National Education Software – *fastdir.com*

"Craig has a keen understanding of the challenges that family-owned businesses face, especially transitioning to the next generation. This book focuses on efforts to help all the employees succeed."

Emily Allman-Thiel (G2), Controller, AMS Controls
Global Electronics Integrator – *amscontrols.com*

"This book can easily be read in one sitting. It's straightforward and respectful of the reader's busy schedule. Yet it's got many great ideas! There are a lot of management books on the market. This is a gem!"

Clark Reed (G3), President, Reed Rubber Products
National Manufacturer – *reedrubberproducts.com*

"A must read for everyone involved in a family business! Your practical guidance to unique business threats brings harmony and opportunity to potentially divisive family business decisions. Excellent!"

Pat Mooney (G2), President, Footwear Unlimited
International Importer – *footwearunlimited.com*

"Excellent! With so many management books on the market this one truly is simple and concise. It's a refreshing guide for helping family members work together as a team in reaching their goals."

Penny Wagner (G2), Vice President, Wagner Portrait Group
Regional Photography - *wagnerportraitgroup.com*

Printed in the United States of America
10 9 8 7 6 5 4 3 2 1

ISBN: 978-1-893308-14-5

Optim Consulting Group

optimgroupusa.com

St. Louis, Missouri

*Dedicated to Kelly, Steven and Jennifer
as their journey continues...*

Table of Contents

Tips

Purpose

The *Business Person's Handbook* consists of a series of practical tips that address real-world issues facing today's businessperson. The purpose is to provide concise, thought-provoking perspectives that will lead to timely, positive solutions for you and your team.

Personal Assessments
Who Are We

Any family business is, by definition, an interactive enterprise. The quality of the interaction determines the success or failure of the enterprise. For a family business to thrive, each person taking part in interactions within the business needs to be able to answer the question *WHO ARE WE?*

This is a critical inquiry for all contributors to all businesses, but it is a particularly important one for a family-owned business, where special challenges to collaboration exist. Some people assume that members of a family business already know who they're working with. Often this is not the case. In fact, answering the *WHO ARE WE?* question is actually more difficult for family businesses than it is for other companies, because patterns of interaction can become ingrained over the years.

One of the best ways to begin to answer the question *WHO ARE WE?* is for all the key members of the management team to commit to a standard behavioral assessment tool, conduct the assessment and then discuss the results together as a group. There are a number of excellent assessments available. Which one is ultimately selected is up to management.

Discussing and evaluating this type of assessment can go a long way toward improving communication between first-generation (G1) contributors, such as the founder of the company, and second-generation (G2) contributors, such as the adult children who report to the founder. Just as important, the assessment can increase respect and good will across the generations and management team.

"As far as possible without surrender, be on good terms with all persons."

Max Ehrmann

Some people say they "don't believe in personality assessments." Yet if you were to ask these same people: "Just between you and me, is there anyone you have a little trouble getting along with around the office?" the answer would usually be "Yes." Not only that, you would probably find that the person has plenty to say about the various problems.

In fact, if you were to listen long enough to the many points of aggravation, you might be tempted to conclude that these two people simply were not compatible, that they should not be working together in the same room or even in the same building. Yet this is rarely the case.

What's much more common is that they simply haven't developed good skills for interacting with each other, because they haven't yet answered the question *WHO ARE WE?* And that's all an assessment does. It answers that question and begins that discussion.

Exploring the *WHO ARE WE* question gives people tools for interacting much more effectively with each other, so that they communicate better and get more done.

Most assessment tools would agree on the existence of four basic behavior traits. It's very likely that you "lean on" one of these four traits more during your typical working day than you do on the other three. Read the list of statements below carefully, and then ask yourself which one of these four behavior styles seems to come most naturally to you.

1. Personal Power: I can easily contribute by *overcoming opposition* in order to make things happen. (Yes/No)

2. People Power: I can easily contribute by *influencing or persuading* other people. (Yes/No)

3. Team Power: I can easily contribute by *cooperating with others* as part of a team effort. (Yes/No)

4. Quality Power: I can easily contribute by *analyzing to insure quality and accuracy*, and particularly by spotting mistakes or inconsistencies. (Yes/No)

Of course, people are complex, and they do have more than one dimension. It is definitely possible to do more than one of these things. And there is a lot more to knowing you than knowing which of these statements it was easiest for you to say "Yes" to.

Yet you do have a preference here. Everyone working in your family business does. Everyone has predispositions, certain ways of doing things and looking at things. It is particularly important for members of a family business to know each other's predispositions -- so they can make adaptations, stay on good terms and work harmoniously.

The reality is, sometimes having a working relationship with a family member can be extremely stressful. Understanding *WHO WE ARE* is a critical part of managing that workplace stress. This is because the stakes are so much higher for these businesses. When the relationship in a family business is solid, it's really solid. But when there are problems in the relationship, they tend to be big problems. That's why adaptations based on understanding your own behavior style, and the behavior styles of others are so important.

Here's a real-life situation that plays out in plenty of family businesses. The company founder (we'll call him Dad) has a habit of striding briskly into the office of the head of accounting (we'll call her Daughter) to ask a question. One morning he barges in as usual, and then talks. Daughter is busy studying a spreadsheet carefully, but Dad wants to get the answer to a question he needs to address. As usual, it's an urgent question.

These exchanges never seem to go well for either Dad or Daughter. There is always an underlying tension, and Daughter feels resentments about these exchanges that are hard for her to describe or resolve. For his part, Dad only vaguely realizes that something is wrong, and that realization passes pretty quickly. He's got a question he needs answered, and he keeps pushing until he gets what he's looking for. Sometimes he feels Daughter is too "emotional" about being interrupted, and that she "loses focus" too easily.

In a scenario like this, Daughter may say or think something like this: "I love my Dad, but I just don't know how much longer I can keep working with him. We just get on each other's last nerve. I think I need to start looking for another job."

Maybe she does, maybe she doesn't. A very simple adaptation can make life much easier for each of them, but it can only happen once they both begin to understand *WHO WE ARE*.

Suppose we ran a behavioral assessment. We would probably find that Dad, like a lot of founder/entrepreneurs, answered "Yes" to question 1:

1. Personal Power: I can easily contribute by *overcoming opposition* in order to make things happen. (Yes/No)

Daughter, like a lot of effective accounting professionals, answered "Yes" to question 4:

4. Quality Power: I can easily contribute by *analyzing to insure quality and accuracy*, and particularly by spotting mistakes or inconsistencies. (Yes/No)

So what's the adaptation? Consider: If Dad knocks on Daughter's door, then waits three full seconds, instead of just barging into her office the whole dynamic of the relationship changes. This gives Daughter a chance to disengage from her spreadsheet (or whatever she's analyzing), and focus her full attention on what he's asking. The two aren't stepping on each other's toes anymore. And they can be there for each other.

It works. Why? Because both Dad and Daughter know *WHO WE ARE*. And knowing that, they can identify and avoid the interaction problem altogether. If we don't know *WHO WE ARE*, we may decide that this kind of adaptation is impossible. Usually, though, it isn't!

Understanding *WHO WE ARE* is essential to harmonious, productive working relationships, especially in family-owned businesses. Intelligent adaptation can save working relationships -- and family relationships. There is no substitute for actually taking the personal behavior assessment and studying the results as a team. It takes less time than you think and it saves time and aggravation.

**"A clever person solves a problem.
A wise person avoids it."**

Albert Einstein

Goal Setting
Company Versus Personal

The role of goal (objective) setting has become significantly more important in all aspects of life during the past few years, particularly in family-owned businesses. For instance, most of us want to achieve balance between our home and our work life. Achieving this goal can be a challenge for everyone, but it is a particularly difficult one for many employees of family-owned businesses.

At home, we are likely to set goals that, if achieved, would allow us to spend more quality time with our loved ones, and we also want time for personal activities such as hobbies, sports, traveling and volunteer work. On the job, we may strive harder than ever before to outperform the competition, while at the same time attempting to satisfy our customers' needs. We may set goals related to offering better products and services at even lower prices, and to securing greater market share, revenues and profitability.

Making sure that personal and company goals match up has become paramount to personal success, and to the success of the family business. A goal is a quantifiable benchmark. It provides a gauge for measuring present and future performance. And it is a stimulus for accomplishment, because it offers a sense of purpose.

The proper balance of personal and corporate goals will provide greater harmony and greater opportunity, so that all your goals can be realized. You cannot afford to delay, however, because each lost or misspent moment or day will result in some form of additional cost to yourself and/or your company.

"CARPE DIEM"
Seize the day.

Horace

Mission Statement

Management can establish corporate goals at any time and for any reason. However, for any goal to result in success, management must fully understand the goal's intent and its implications in relation to the company mission. This is especially true in the family-owned business.

The first step is for management to recognize the difference between a corporate mission statement and the corporate goal. The former is more intangible in nature. It is a "vision" of the future of the family-owned business. It should conjure up feelings of excitement and pleasure. It should define why the company exists. It should provide direction for the company for years to come, and should be shared both internally and externally.

For example, ABC Company's mission might be "To become the leading supplier of data management and customer relationship applications to nonprofit organizations throughout the state."

The corporate goal is more concrete than the mission statement. While the experience of actually accomplishing the goal should certainly conjure up feelings of excitement and pleasure, the daily movement of working towards a goal is more operational in scope. This goal is more short-term in nature than the mission statement. It is primarily designed to be shared with employees and stakeholders. At a family-owned business, one critical criteria for corporate goals is that they motivate both G1 and G2 employees to attain them!

Traditionally, corporate goals have related to three primary benchmarks: market share, revenues and profitability. In recent years, customer metrics have been added to this list.

Goals are typically set for time frames ranging between six months and three years. In the case of ABC Company, its six-month goal might be to improve customer satisfaction ratings to 90%. The twelve-month goal might be to increase revenues by 25% and pretax profitability to 15% with a 40% market share.

Many family-owned businesses take ABC's approach, and pursue more than one corporate goal simultaneously. Goals can target different benchmarks, as these do, and need not be mutually exclusive.

Personal Goals

While examining corporate goals, the management team of a family business should simultaneously establish and/or review their individual personal goals. Frequently, the firm's goals are a mirror of management's personal philosophies.

For instance, suppose ABC Company's president once worked for a firm that required substantial overnight travel. This proved problematic, because he felt cheated from spending quality time with his family. He vowed never to subject his employees the same hardship if and when he launched his own company. Consequently, he restricted ABC's geographic growth to the state where the business is located, so that overnight travel would be limited. He also made a strategic decision to focus the company's resources on a single popular software product that is directly relevant only to non-profit organizations in his home state.

The potential disconnect between G1 and G2 players is easy to make out here. Suppose the president's son envisions a much more aggressive short-term growth track for the company, and wants to offer multiple new software applications and expand operations out-of-state. In this case, a generational divide exists between G1 and G2, and must be examined and resolved before "buy-in" on personal or organizational goals can be attained.

When the family owned business's management team consists of more than one person, the first step in goal-setting should entail the completion of individual personality profiles. While general personality traits may already be known, an outside facilitator can assist in documenting the specific traits that should be discussed in an open forum. This will aid in the creation of common ground and give a sense of respect for the ways other members of the team, whether family members or not, will go about working to obtain an objective.

The second step is for the facilitator to assist the management team in establishing and or reviewing personal goals. The group will begin by determining which time frame should be chosen. Ideally, the time frame selected will include short-term (6 to 12 months), medium-term (1 to 3 years) and long-term (over three years) goals. Then members should share their goals, which should all be recorded in on the left side of the flip chart or chalkboard for each time frame.

Once everyone has identified his or her personal goals, the facilitator will list the business goals in column form on the right side of the flip chart or chalkboard.

The next step is to compare each individual's personal and business goals for each time frame. The partners of a local family-owned wholesale distributor shared their goals as follows. Note that Person A is a G1 contributor with an emphasis on Personal Power, while Person B is a G2 contributor with more of an emphasis on Team Power.

Person A (G1 – Personal Power)

Time Frame	Personal	Business
6 months	African safari	Large new office
12 months	Buy condo in London 20% salary increase	20% revenue increase 20% profit increase
36 months	Buy a plane Autobiography	50% revenue increase 50% profit increase

Partner B (G2 – Team Power)

Time Frame	Personal	Business
6 months	Leadership training	Team building retreat
12 months	Music Lessons 10% salary increase	10% revenue increase 10% profit increase
36 months	1 month vacation Chair non-profit	Profit sharing program Employee sabaticals

Resolution

This was the first time in years that these two colleagues had actually shared their personal and business goals. Tremendous tensions had developed among them during this period of time; each of them had felt slighted by the other. Not until they openly discussed their personality profiles and their current goals did they recognize that they were on different paths. Once they had a clear understanding of each other, mutual respect was reestablished. They have since unified their efforts in reaching not only their individual goals but also in working together towards realizing their family business's corporate mission.

Summary

In conclusion, goal (objective) setting is important in all aspects of our lives. Whether it is personally or organizationally related, goal-setting is paramount to success. In terms of the family-owned business, the firm's goals are frequently a mirror of management's personal philosophies, and the possibility of goal-related conflict based on personality or on generational issues is significant. For this reason, it is imperative that all the members of the family business's management team simultaneously establish and or review their business and personal goals as a team.

There's no better way to unify efforts and keep everyone on the same path than to discuss goals. Goals may be seen from very different perspectives, but when they are discussed and analyzed together, they tend to identify quite similar objectives for all parties involved.

**"You cannot dream yourself
into a character; you must hammer
and forge yourself into one."**

James A. Froude

Corporate Mission
Common Purpose

Most family-owned companies do not have a written mission statement. This is unfortunate, because family-owned businesses have a GREATER strategic need to create and circulate a clear, compelling, unifying company mission than other businesses.

Why? Because of the more complex patterns of relationship and behavior in these companies, because of the potential divide between family employees and other employees, and because of the possibility of starkly differing perspectives between G1 and G2 contributors on the issue of "where we're going." All of this makes the answer to the question "What's our mission?" more important for a family-owned company.

Envision your personal dream vacation. Is it exploring the pyramids of Egypt? Sailing in the Caribbean? Taking a trip with the family to Disney World? Playing alongside your heroes on a sports fantasy team? Whatever your dream might be, it undoubtedly conjures up feelings of excitement and pleasure.

Of course, the dream may seem hazy at first, because you may not have a clear picture. But the more you place yourself in that dream, the more clear and focused it becomes. And in time, you realize that with the proper motivation and commitment, the dream vacation can become a reality.

Your company mission statement is analogous to your dream vacation! It should represent a "vision" of the future. It should conjure up feelings of excitement and pleasure. It should become a well focused picture in your mind. Your company mission should represent a far-reaching goal that can inspire everyone in the family-owned business to unify and turn the dream into reality.

**"Dream manfully and nobly,
and thy dreams shall be prophets."**

Edward George Bulwer-Lytton

Are mission statements meaningful? Absolutely, if properly conceived and executed! Otherwise, the mission statement will become a worthless document. In fact, it can actually damage the company if it results in negative feelings among the family business's rank and file.

Reasons for Failure

There is no published data that rank by percentage the failure-success level of mission statement utilization in family-owned businesses. However, there is an endless list of examples that reflect both scenarios. Let's first examine some of the reasons stated for the failure of mission statements, either in design or execution.

One of the most common reasons for mission statement failure is that a business owner or a management team develops the mission statement in a vacuum. They decide that having a mission statement would be "cool." However, no effort is made to consider the employees' perspective. Management develops its new revelation in a vacuum, and announces the concept at a staff meeting. And it fails.

In the vacuum syndrome, management misses the opportunity to gain insights from the rest of the organization. What if employees could have warned management that the entire marketplace was beginning to change, and that this would impact the company mission? What if a marketing person had not yet communicated that the competition had developed a new technology that might make current products obsolete? Or that new environmental laws had unexpectedly created a problem that will force clients away from the company's current product line?

Publication Syndrome

The publication syndrome occurs when the creator(s) of the mission statement are looking to publish a book. The mission statement soon loses purpose as it grows into a novel-length tome. The vision of a dream vacation is no longer a simple picture. The author includes every detail possible. The simple road map becomes an exhaustive itinerary including every road and highway, rest stop, restaurant, tourist activity and sleeping accommodations for the entire vacation.

In the publication syndrome, management loses sight of the mission. In fact, they become wrapped up in details that are irrelevant to the mission. They write a book. The mission statement should not be complex. It should be easily understood, easy to remember by the entire organization, and less than 50 words in length.

The nearsighted syndrome occurs when management decides that implementing a mission statement will be a great way to quickly motivate the rank and file about some short-term issue. This could be as simple as boosting revenues or profits by the next quarter. Management doesn't care who is involved in the mission's development, as long as it is rolled-out promptly.

The problem here is that the mission statement is short-term oriented, rather than long-term oriented. It focuses on next quarter's revenues or profits, and not on the future mission of the organization. The mission statement should never be used as an artificial, short-term motivating device. When it is used for this purpose, negative feedback from the employees is to be expected, particularly if they already feel management is manipulating them.

Impossible Dream Syndrome

The impossible dream syndrome does not limit employee involvement in the creation of the mission statement. It is concise, motivating and well received by the entire team. However, this syndrome goes beyond being "almost" impossible. It is impossible!

The consequence of the impossible dream syndrome is that the mission will quickly be deemed impractical, and apathy sets in. There will be no true motivation for realizing the mission. This occurred when a small manufacturer released the following mission statement after consulting its employees: "We will become the world's largest supplier of industrial valves." Very quickly, the group realized the statement was impractical and held no value for them.

This syndrome is a particularly serious obstacle for family-owned businesses, where there may be very different perceptions between G1 and G2 participants about what is possible and what isn't.

The Right Approach

Ideally, the mission statement should define why your company exists. Several fundamental questions must be answered:

▶ What is our business?

▶ Who is our customer?

▶ What is our customer's perception of value?

▶ How will our business be shaped in the future?

Management guru Peter Drucker, said that the mission statement should also be shaped by the following five critical factors:

Critical Factors

I. Your company's history of direction and achievements.

Do not shift radically from your company's historical focus unless this strategic choice is necessitated by a major event such as a change in technology, economics, government regulation, demographics, society or competition.

Example: Netflix adopted a streaming-video model when it became apparent that its DVD-distribution model would not satisfy all its customers needs. To remain a viable business, Netflix became a streaming video-on-demand supplier as well.

II. The current preference of your company's ownership and management.

Personal preferences of your family-owned company's leadership will obviously have an impact on significant corporate strategy and decisions.

Example: An equipment distributor decided to service only the local marketplace because senior management had no desire to incur overnight travel.

III. Influences of your market environment.

Threats or opportunities occur that may have an impact on your firm's performance.

Example: The state school system has mandated that on-line education become an integral component of future programs. This presents a wide-open market with new business opportunities.

IV. Limits of your company's resources.

You have a limited amount of time and dollars. You must determine where and how these are to be utilized.

Example: Funds are not available for a regional grocery chain to expand nationally.

V. Your company's distinctive competencies.

Your firm delivers products and/or services which satisfy certain customers' needs. You must maintain focus and not deviate too far from your core strengths.

Example: Enterprise Rent-A-Car could rent planes, but their strength is managing vehicles.

Clear Missions

The following mission statements fulfill the criteria just described:

Wagner Portrait Group's mission is to provide a superior image with an exceptional experience dedicated to the unique needs of our customer and their entire community.

AMS Control's mission is to provide world-class engineered solutions – including production management software and integrated machine controls – that optimize the operations of manufacturers in the metal profiling industry and provide a fair return on investment.

Summary

In summary, the mission statement should be as motivating as the "dream vacation." Its creation should include input from all parts of the company team. It should emphasize market rather than product. The goals it describes should be challenging to obtain, but not impossible. It should unite management and employees, family members and non-family members, G1 and G2. It should provide direction for the company for years to come. It should be flexible enough to change as the need arises. It should be shared with customers and prospects. And it should be less than 50 words in length.

"Lift where you stand."

Edward Everett Hale

Employee Partnership
A True Benefit

There has been much talk in recent years about internal and external customers. These discussions indicate that the employee's needs should be recognized as being just as important to the organization as the needs of the ultimate customer.

These discussions are important to family-owned businesses that are committed to strong growth, because there is a strong correlation between those companies who develop better partnerships with their employees and those companies who have more satisfied customers.

The potential for such partnerships with employees at family-owned businesses is often greater than at other companies, because of the shared sense of commitment in these businesses.

A comprehensive plan to create greater employee satisfaction can provide a road map to increased financial success for both the company and its employees. The best modern example of this might be Walmart, which began as a family business when the late Sam Walton purchased a Bentonville, Arkansas store with the help of a loan from his father-in-law. Today, the firm's chairman of the board is S. Robson Walton, eldest son of Sam Walton.

Sam Walton believed his company's success was a direct result of how its employees, referred to as associates, were inherently treated within the organization. Walton preached, "The way management treats the associates is exactly how the associates will then treat the customer. And if the customer is treated well, they will return again and again, and that is where real profits lie, not in trying to drag strangers in for one-time purchases."

**"Throw your heart over the fence
and the rest will follow."**

Norman Vincent Peale

Size Is Not An Issue

There are three key issues about Sam Walton's "internal customers" or associates philosophy that are of particular interest to family-owned businesses.

First, company size and geographic dispersion should not be determinants in establishing a true partnership philosophy throughout your organization.

For example, despite its incredible size and broad geographic dispersion, Walmart has overcome the challenge of dispensing a partnership philosophy throughout its more than two million employee, international organization. Relatively speaking, the smaller-sized business should find the process much easier to execute.

Human Consideration

Second, Walton advocated: that, "partnership involves money—which is critical to any business relationship—but it also involves basic human consideration, such as respect."

The "human consideration" often has a significant impact on the financial success for both the company and employees. More satisfied employees lead to more satisfied customers, and more satisfied customers lead to more positive results.

The first step in developing a partnership with your employees is to eliminate the "us against them" attitude that affects too many family-owned businesses, often as a result of divisions between family and non-family contributors, or between G1 and G2 team members. To overcome these divisions, take to heart the following list of recommendations.

Partnership Building

▶ Refer to your people by some phrase other than "employees." Know their names. Use empowering descriptions such as associates, partners or team members.

▶ Confirm that your team understands the company mission and goals. They need to know the target before they aim.

▶ Hire people who embrace the "shared mission" attitude. There must be a unified commitment from the entire team.

▶ Support and promote team members as they execute the "shared mission" attitude.

▶ Let the associates know what is expected of them. They will surprise you with their commitment and ingenuity in achieving it.

▶ Listen to your associates. Ask them how they can be better served so that they can better serve the customer. Take action on the best ideas, and acknowledge those who provided them.

▶ Keep close to your external customers so you know what they desire and how well your team is delivering on that desire.

▶ Inform your associates regularly on their performance. Feedback provides a mechanism for their continuous improvement.

▶ Praise people in public and criticize them in private. Praise should be based on positive business results or it will not be taken seriously. Criticism should be constructive.

▶ Inform your associates regularly on the specifics of the company's performance. They need a benchmark to gauge success.

Walton's third issue focuses on the money aspect of the associate partnership. There are numerous financial benefits to be realized from truly nurturing such a relationship.

First, know that if you elect to create a more pleasant work environment for your team, it has been proven that your associates' attitudes will be positively influenced. While it is difficult to measure the specific payback of such an investment, positive attitudes by the team generally translates into greater productivity and profitability.

Second, employee turnover is typically lower in those organizations that empower employees to function as if they were shareholders. This translates into measurable cost savings for your organization due to lower turnover expense. Some examples include the following.

Reduced Turnover Equals Savings

▶ Administrative costs associated with recruiting and hiring will be greatly reduced as turnover slows down.

▶ Management and associates will spend less time in the employee recruiting, interviewing, orientation and training steps.

▶ Learning curves will decrease if fewer positions are vacated and filled by new associates.

▶ Lost knowledge and experience of departing associates will be greatly reduced.

Unhappy associates can have a major impact on your bottom line. Quite simply, they can and will make your customers unhappy. Tension related conflicts about the vision or mission of the company can be a factor here, which is one reason why gaining input and commitment from all the company's constituencies, and particularly from both G1 and G2, is so critical to retaining the family-owned company's customers.

Studies, including those done by The Technical Assistance Project (TARP) indicate that 65% of the unhappy customers who quit doing business with a particular company do so for reasons other than poor product or price. Service is considered the overriding factor. In other words, the supplier did a poor job of providing service during some point of the transaction causing the customer to defect.

This becomes an important consideration when one realizes how difficult and expensive it can be to replace lost customers. It is frequently pointed out that the cost of replacing a lost customer is six to nine times as great as it is in keeping a current customer. If only we listened more closely!

Entrepreneurial Partners

Ray Higgins, owner of Fritz's Custard, has taken Sam Walton's partnership philosophy to heart. Higgins attributes the dramatic growth of his small firm to his team of designated "co-workers." These individuals truly feel they are vested in the partnership of the organization because they are empowered to function as if they were shareholders. They flourish within an entrepreneurial environment.

Higgins says, "You need good people to grow. They must run the business as if it were their own. I do not run our facility, but rather, everybody contributes as part of the team."

Throughout the year, Higgins' team receives feedback. The feedback is not a one-time event. It is part of an ongoing process that Higgins has implemented. There is an annual awards dinner, and, every few years, a team vacation trip. Higgins (G1) has successfully transposed this philosophy onto his daughter Lindsay (G2) who now runs the daily operations of the family company.

Remember what Sam Walton preached? It's worth reading twice. "The way management treats the associates is exactly how the associates will then treat the customers. And if the customers are treated well, they will return again and again, and that is where real profits lie, not in trying to drag strangers in for one-time purchases."

Walton must have known something. He built one of the largest and most successful firms in the world under the partnership concept. Obviously, the internal customer really does matter.

**"To get the best out of a man
go to what is best in him."**

Daniel Considine

Employee Feedback
A Direct Link

Employee feedback is a direct link to success for your family-owned business. So often in our efforts to satisfy customer needs, we seem to bypass one of our greatest assets – that of our employees, our "internal customers."

Whether the employees are referred to as associates, partners or team members, these individuals represent the ultimate link between management and the customer. They are one the critical component in the value chain that is capable of providing feedback from both the customer, and themselves, on how well your organization is performing in delivering its products and services to the marketplace.

Remember that your family business exists to satisfy customers' needs, and that those needs invariably change over time. You must continuously probe to determine where there is pain or passion. These are the two drivers that create the need. Whenever your customer has pain there is a need for relief. And whenever your customer has passion, there is a need to fulfill a desire. In either case, your quick and accurate assessment spells opportunity.

By listening to your associates, you gain first-hand knowledge as to how you are performing in satisfying your customers' needs. These perceptions are critical for the success of your company in realizing its mission and goals.

**"Praise the bridge
that carried you over."**

George Colman
The Younger

Feedback Mechanisms

There are numerous methods for staying in touch with your associates. The simplest is to establish an ongoing process for them to share information with management and their fellow team members. These processes must be equally open to family member employees and non-family employees. They must be equally open to G1 contributors and G2 contributors. And all the feedback must be evaluated carefully, on a consistent basis.

As opportunities and issues of concern surface, the associate should be made to feel comfortable in delivering information and opinions within the organization. The ability to communicate openly, regardless of whether or not one is related to the family that owns the business, regardless of whether or not one is G1 or G2, is absolutely essential. This freedom will ensure that everyone feels his or her input will be considered and is extremely important to the growth of your family business.

The ongoing feedback mechanisms can be designed in a free-flowing format, or structured on a more formal basis. For example, written messages, oral, email or some other method may be used as the associate sees fit. Management can prioritize these communications in such a way that some issues can be discussed spontaneously, while others can be addressed on a more formal basis, such as scheduling meeting times.

In addition to this ongoing feedback from associates, a formal audit of perceptions under the guidance of an outside facilitator can provide valuable information. The focus can be on particular aspects of the family-owned business's performance, or can be broader in scope.

Known as the Employee Perception Survey, the audit can either be completed by all the associates or by a sampling of those in various parts of the company. This survey has become an integral tool in many a company's quest to gain competitive superiority.

Employee Perception Survey

The intent of the Employee Perception Survey is to gain a better understanding of the associates' perceptions about issues known to be important for the smooth and efficient management of the family-owned business. The survey provides feedback regarding those "critical issues" that will produce an accurate picture about where to focus the company's improvement energies as it strives to satisfy its customers and fulfill its own mission and goals.

The survey should be designed to meet the particular needs of any organization. The following sections have proven valuable in covering the core issues affecting most companies.

Section One

The first part of the survey is to ask the associates to rank various issues (usually about 20) from most important to least important for the long-term success of the family-owned business. These are ranked in a format such as from number 1 (most important) to number 20 (least important). Each number should be used only once. Typical issues include:

▶ Company mission and goals

▶ Company culture and team effort

▶ Rewards and recognition

▶ Product and service quality

The next step is to identify which of the rated issues offer the greatest current opportunity for improvement. Once again, this is based on how the associate perceives the situation.

Section Two

Section two consists of a series of open-ended questions designed specifically for the family-owed business. A common thread among these questions is the issue of how the associates perceive their personal roles relative to the company mission. Of equal importance is the question of what role the associates perceive their superiors play (or should play) within the organization. Questions for this section might include:

▶ What is your role within the organization?

▶ Do you fulfill your role?

▶ What is the role of your boss?

▶ Does your boss fulfill the role as described?

▶ How might your roles better assist you both in helping the company realize its mission and goals?

Section Three

The primary purpose of this section is to identify the strengths and weaknesses of the company as perceived by the associates. There are several questions that should be answered here, including the following:

▶ Do the associates agree by department, division and/or universally on the strengths and weaknesses of the company? If not, why?

▶ What can be done to improve the company's performance in satisfying its customers as well as in realizing its mission and goals?

The employee - associate, partner or team player is the ultimate link between management and the customer. He or she is the one component in the value chain capable of providing feedback from the customer, as well as personal feedback on how well the company is performing.

The customized Employee Perception Survey offers an excellent method for gathering this critical information. It should be administered fairly, providing equal access to all team members, and should be considered an integral tool for the family-owned company in reaching competitive superiority.

"You can exert no influence if you are not susceptible to influence."

C. G. Jung

Organizational Chart
Who and Where

**Who *is* doing what and who *should be*
doing what in your family business?**

Whether your company is a small one in which
family members are out on the front lines, serving
customers and doing plenty of face-to-face
interaction, or a larger enterprise where the family
members all occupy leadership positions on the
senior management team, you should make a point
of periodically reviewing your organizational chart
also known as an "org chart." This tip will help you
to conduct a careful review of that document (or
create one if you have not yet done so).

What Is an Org Chart?

The dictionary tells us that an org chart is "a diagram that shows the structure of an organization and the relationships and relative ranks of its parts and positions/jobs." In essence, it's a visual breakdown of who's doing what within your family owned-business. An effective org chart always answers two questions.

▶ Who is doing what?

▶ Who reports to whom?

Here is an example of a traditional org chart:

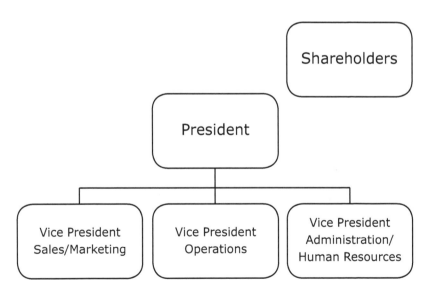

**"You may be a disappointment
if you fail, but you are doomed
if you don't try."**

Beverly Sills

If you have not yet broken down the operational responsibilities of your family-owned business into a visual aid that everyone can see and understand, now is the time to start. The org chart tells you what your process looks like now. You cannot improve a process if you have not yet identified what its component parts do, and how they interact with each other!

Think of your initial draft of the org chart as a "snapshot" that shows who has what formal responsibility, and who is responsible for a given work area. Use the chart just shared as a model for a first draft of your org chart. And then be ready to update and revise that org chart based on what you will be learning here.

Please do not continue with this tip until you have a first draft of your org chart complete and in your hands. The org chart can be executed very simply. If you want, you can use a simple sketch of boxes and titles on a single sheet of paper to get started.

The Reality Check

Whatever version of your org chart you are now looking at -- whether it is your first draft or your fiftieth -- you must subject it to a reality check at least once a year. Most companies do not do this. If you have not critically reviewed your org chart in the past twelve months to make sure that it makes strategic sense for your business, you should do that right now.

This strategic reassessment is very different from the "snapshot" mentioned earlier. Now, you are not asking "what is" but rather "what should be." Inevitably, in the family-owned businesses, it turns out that certain people who show up on the org chart do not represent an optimal fit for the jobs that they have. It is also quite common for people to have job titles that do not reflect what they really do all day long. Be honest. Where do you see instances of that on the org chart? What should be done about that?

When people aren't in the right spot on the org chart, or when they have jobs that they don't do well, you erode the partnership with the rest of the employees in the company. This is particularly common in family-based businesses, where a G1 has placed a G2 in a spot on the org chart that does not reflect the daily reality of the person's actual capacity for contributing to the company. When this happens, all the processes in the company are at risk of being degraded.

After the reality check, senior management must ask: How does this chart need to change in order to best serve the company?

Company or a Job?

A fundamental question is: "Do you have a company or do you have a job?" This is a critical question that eventually confronts the management team of just about every family-owned business.

Michael Gerber in his acclaimed book entitled the EMyth suggested: "There is no right or wrong if you have a company or a job. Just be truthful to yourself in identifying what you do have versus what you want and act accordingly."

In either case, how strong are your processes and systems? What happens if key people leave? What happens if someone dies or is incapacitated? For most family-owned companies, the answer is: "We're in trouble." That's a sign that you don't yet have a company -- you have a job.

Getting the org chart right is the essential starting point for getting the right processes and systems in place in the company! In fact, org chart problems are a big reason why so many family-owned companies are worth less than the founders (G1) think. There is no process, no system to replicate (or sell!) the company.

Deep conflicts can unfold in family-owned businesses over the questions of what job titles people have and who gets paid for doing what. People in these businesses often ask themselves: Is so-and-so getting more credit than I am, or getting paid more than I am?

These are emotional issues, and they often tie into complex family relationship issues. They often take the focus away from tougher questions that may actually be more important, such as:

▶ Who would we put where if we were starting this business over from scratch?

▶ Who should be someplace else?

▶ Who should be in a different role entirely?

▶ Who should be out-placed into another job somewhere else?

Review these questions annually—at the very least. As you do, bear in mind that the outplacement option is one that can solve many problems. At one family-owned company, a G2 manager decided to take advantage of the outplacement idea after it had been raised by a private consultant. In his new job, he ended up working 45 hours a week instead of the 55-60 hours he had been working at the company his father had founded, and making 30% more income! The company he left behind was eventually running more smoothly. Everybody was happier -- although the manager's father had been skeptical of the outplacement option, and would never have suggested it on his own.

In these situations, there is often a "family curse" that G2 and G3 contributors face in terms of a G1 founder's expectations. Many G2s and G3s feel a burden of obligation to fulfill the expectations of a parent -- even if that parent is now dead! Sometimes, the weight of parental expectations simply has to be removed if the company is to move forward.

In re-evaluating your org chart, look closely at compensation as well as fit, and remember that in a family-owned business, compensation comes in three varieties:

Ownership Distribution (which is for financial stakeholders, whether or not they are involved in running the business)

Employee Compensation (which must be both market-based and performance-based, reflecting the person's actual ability to fulfill the responsibilities of the job, when compared to the rest of the employment pool)

Employee Bonus (which should be a payment based on reaching specific performance targets)

These are all distinct income sources, and it is not a given that someone who is receiving income from one source should also receive income from either of the other sources.

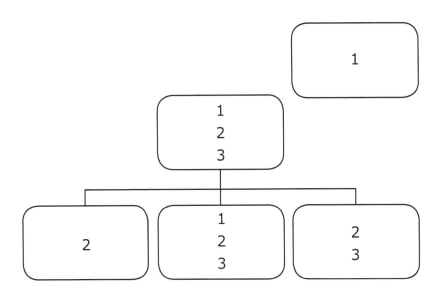

1 Ownership Distribution

2 Employee Compensation

3 Employee Bonus

Summary

You want a "real world" org chart that closes the gap between processes that don't produce good results and processes that do. This may be a slow transition, but it is essential that it begin, and that it be repeated at least annually.

Look critically at both the processes and the results! Then reboot your family business.

"After a good dinner one can forgive anybody, even one's own relations."

Oscar Wilde

tip 7

Building Strengths
Education and Coaching

If the people who work within a family-owned business are not growing, developing and adapting to change in a healthy way, then the company itself will not grow and develop and adapt in a healthy way. If you want your company to keep up in the marketplace, you have to invest in the education and coaching that will support your team's ability to keep up.

These days, there's a lot to keep up with and a lot to adapt to. If you operate a business today, you operate within a constantly changing marketplace, one that is reinventing itself week by week and day by day in dynamic new ways. You and your team must adapt to new consumer trends, new technologies and new ways of interacting if you want your business to succeed.

If you have any doubts about that ever-changing reality, or about the need for an ever-changing response to it, then consider this: **If you can remember the year 2003, when George W. Bush was president, then you remember a world in which there was no Facebook, no YouTube, no LinkedIn and no Twitter.** In the years since, businesses of all sizes have had to adapt to these powerful communication channels -- as marketing platforms, as sales resources, as customer service forums and as public relations vehicles. In the years since 2003, in fact, all four of those strategic business activities have coalesced and overlapped, thanks to the massive influence of these and other social media channels! Companies that fail to adapt to such changes experience slower-than-optimum growth -- or even fail.

By the time you read these words, some new piece of technology, some new application, some new communication tool will be poised to transform the marketplace realities faced by whole industries, probably yours. If you expect to be able to compete, all your family business's people had better be growing and improving, too.

"There is nothing noble in being superior to your fellow man; true nobility is being superior to your former self."

Ernest Hemingway

If your people aren't being challenged to grow and excel, then your systems and processes are not as strong as they could be. And remember, if you have no viable system, no viable process, then your company is worth far less than you think!

Unfortunately, many family-owned companies do not have good systems in place and the people who work at those companies haven't been coached to be managers of their own destiny. Often, this is a G1/G2 issue. In many cases, the first-generation patriarch or matriarch simply doesn't trust the kids, and is not supporting their growth and development. G1 players often talk eloquently about building a business for the second generation, but quite frequently the reality experienced by second-generation contributors is very different.

What matters is not whether or not the founder talks about leaving a positive legacy for the family in the future, but whether the actions he or she undertakes support that goal. The actions, after all, speak much louder than the words. If someone speaks eloquently about building a business "for the kids" but is actually using it to corral them, then something needs to change. The second generation

-- the future of the company -- cannot be positioned for growth if they're pigeonholed in some stereotype about what they are and aren't capable of achieving!

At most family-owned businesses, there is an urgent and unmet need to create new resources for personal and professional growth. This need is there for all employees, but it is particularly acute among G2 and G3 contributors, who may be stymied by the expectations of a parent or grandparent. To drive this point home to company founders, the following chart may be helpful in planning purposes by plotting out anticipated transition points based upon the age(s) of the G1 / G2 / G3 contributors.

Transition Points

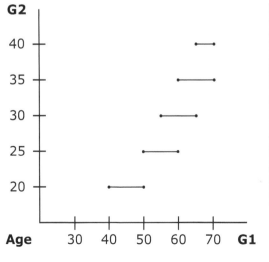

G2	G1
20	40-50
25	50-60
30	55-65
35	60-70
40	65-70

Here, the age ranges of the founder (G1) of the family-owned business are on the horizontal axis and the age ranges of the second-generation (G2) players who should be preparing to take on a greater and more active role in the operation of the company are on the vertical axis. The questions here are obvious: **How robust is the learning track and the career track of the G2 player who is supposed to be in sync with the founder? How close is that person to being ready to step and take over serious responsibilities within the family-owned business?**

For many founders of family-owned businesses, the lack of preparation, personal growth and professional coaching among the members of the second-generation who are simply "waiting in the wings" is a real problem. Waiting is not a strategy for company or personal growth. Woody Allen once said that a relationship is like a shark: It has to keep moving forward in order to stay alive. This is just as true of the relationships within family businesses as it is of romantic relationships! Unless you want your company's growth prospects to resemble those of a dead shark, each and every person in the organization needs to commit to, and be ready to discuss, a plan for personal and professional development. This is particularly important for members of the family-owned business's senior management team.

Development Plan

A unique personal and professional development plan should be an integral part of each and every team member's performance assessment and salary review! If the person is not making progress toward new skills, new capabilities and new career objectives, then the compensation must reflect that -- whether or not the individual is related to the founder of the business. The key questions here are:

▶ What are the career goals of each employee, and particularly each key management figure?

▶ How realistic are those goals?

▶ How often are these goals revised and refined collaboratively?

▶ What is the company doing to support those goals?

▶ What growth trajectory is each key employee on right now?

▶ Specifically, what are the children of the founder doing to move their careers forward and to expand and grow their capabilities?

The Twenty-First Century Ideal

For most of the twentieth century, the dominant career ideal was to get a good job and hold on to it. Now, in the twenty-first century, the ideal for growing family-owned companies (and most other companies) is very different. Now, the goal of everyone in your company, including senior management, should be to work yourself out of a job and prepare yourself for the demands of the next one. This standard definitely DOES include top management!

As we have already seen, markets and technologies can now be expected to change with lightning speed. That means the family-owned business must be poised to adapt quickly, and your skills, capacities and job descriptions must change quickly, too. If you've got the same job you had ten years ago, then there's a problem -- no matter where you are on the org chart!

Summary

No one in the family-owned business today can afford to hold still. If you invest in building up the team's people skills, so everyone can compete going forward, both the business and the family will be better off in both the short and the long term!

"Let him that would move the world first move himself."

Socrates

Business Growth Strategies
The Direction

Contrary to popular belief, the first step in winning a race is not preparing for the race. Instead, the critical first step is CHOOSING the right race in which to compete!

This CHOOSING step is the most essential prerequisite to victory, yet it is often overlooked. This is the heart of developing an effective business growth strategy, and it is perhaps more important for family-owned businesses than any other. Many family-owned businesses neglect or ignore the necessity of developing an effective business growth strategy. Yet this is essential if you wish to "play with the big guys." In this tip, you will learn exactly how the big guys got that way.

The only way for any family business to survive in today's dynamic marketplace is to keep pace with radical social, technological and other disruptive change. This means surpassing your competition in a race of your own choosing. If you're interested in learning how to create your own race, choose a race where you can win, and leave the competition in the dust, then read on.

> **"Behold the turtle.**
> **He makes progress only**
> **when he sticks his neck out."**
>
> James Bryant Conant

Creating Your Own Race

Monitor Your Offering

The first step in creating your own race is to continuously monitor your current product and service offering.

Regardless of whether your family-owned business is a large or small operation, the central question here remains the same: "How are we doing?" It is a critical question, one that the most successful family businesses have asked -- and answered -- for centuries.

Are they satisfying the needs of your customers? Find out. Whether you do so daily, monthly, quarterly or annually, your family-owned business must compare the results with your corporate goals. When the goals for market share, revenues or profits have been met or exceeded, you may consider yourself fortunate to have a short-term competitive advantage. However, this does not bring long-term guarantees and is not a justification for complacency; if you have not reached your goals, the need for action is even more urgent.

The second step in creating your own race is to focus on new business opportunities, otherwise known as growth strategies. The key is to evaluate them relative to market share, revenue and profit potential. **Intensive growth**, the first strategy type represents growth within your company's current line of business. The second growth strategy is **integrative growth**, which means to build or acquire business(s) and/or product(s) within your company's current business line. And the third growth strategy is **diversification**, or adding unrelated business(s) and/or product(s).

Growth Strategies
Intensive Growth
Integrative Growth
Diversification Growth

Let's look at each of these growth strategies in more detail now.

Intensive Growth

Intensive growth has been used most famously in recent years by Apple, as the company *penetrated* outside of its original personal computer market by expanding sales within the education, graphic and music sectors. Apple has further *developed* their market by creating a direct distribution channel with the highly successful Apple Store.

Product development has also increased the revenue and profit stream through the addition of new technologies such as the iPhone, iPad and iPod. These same three intensive strategies can be adapted to your family-owned business.

Intensive Growth
Market Penetration Market Development Product Development

Integrative growth has long been practiced by the automobile manufacturers. For instance, General Motors began *backward integration* by purchasing and building its own component suppliers. However, GM's *forward integration* has been limited because General Motor's vehicles are sold through its network of independent dealerships, which it does not own.

Horizontal integration occurred when General Motors originally purchased several competing manufacturers, thus broadening its product line to include brands like Chevrolet and Cadillac. Here again, precisely the same principles can be applied to any family-owned business pursuing integrative growth.

Integrative Growth
Backward Integration
Forward Integration
Horizontal Integration

Diversification Growth

Diversification growth is used by the direct marketing computer companies such as Dell. There are three different strategies to consider here as well. In Dell's case, the *concentric diversification* strategy occurred with the addition of the laptop computer to their product line, which appealed to current clients and to many first-time buyers.

Horizontal diversification involved offering new, seemingly unrelated technologies to current clients. Dell accomplished this by offering products such as TVs, home theater systems and cameras. A company like Dell might seek *conglomerate diversification*, which involves the purchase of businesses that have no obvious relationship to their current industry, technology or clients. Dell did this when they acquired Quest Software.

Diversification Growth
Concentric Diversification
Horizontal Diversification
Conglomerate Diversification

All companies have ups and downs; the question is not whether these will occur, but how management responds to them. All three companies faced major challenges in the marketplace. Notice that, despite these significant market setbacks, Apple, GM and Dell chose growth strategies that allowed them to choose the right race in which to compete. Your family-owned business can do the same!

Selecting Your "Race" Strategy

Management expert Michael Porter advocates a very structured process for analyzing the marketplace and choosing the right race. The intent is to minimize the risks and maximize the potential payback. Advocating a structured approach, Porter suggests that you carefully consider all the following questions:

▶ What are our core competencies (strengths) and weaknesses? Should these guide our decisions or can we adapt to any opportunity?

▶ What is our competition doing? What are their plans? And how will they react to ours?

▶ What is the potential threat of competitors in the products and markets we are exploring?

▶ What are our suppliers' plans? And how will they react to ours?

▶ What are our clients' plans? And how will they react to ours?

▶ What potential threat exists from substitute products and services?

To maintain a solid growth strategy for your family-owned business, you should review these questions on a quarterly basis, and adjust your plans accordingly in each of the three areas discussed here.

Summary

The rate of change in the marketplace is not going to diminish. If anything, it is going to continue to accelerate. As a result, the larger race -- the race for survival -- is not going to end for your family-owned business. Competitors will come and go, as will industries, technologies, clients and communications platforms. To survive, your company must keep pace.

The very best way to succeed is to surpass your competition by a) monitoring your offerings carefully and b) strategically outmaneuvering your competition in terms of growth strategy by doing a better job of picking races you are likely to win.

"The trick is to make sure you don't die waiting for prosperity to come."

Lee Iocacca

Business Plan
The Implementation

The Chinese sage Lao Tzu may not have realized it two and a half millennia ago, but he was offering important, timeless advice to all family-owned businesses when he wrote:

"If you know the enemy and know yourself, you need not fear the results of a hundred battles."

Let's look at that quote closely. For our purposes, the "knowledge of the enemy and yourself" Lao Tzu mentioned is all your company's formal and informal research, as well as the written plan based on that research and the benchmarks you set up ahead of time for it. The "battle" is the actual implementation of the plan. And the "result of the battle" is your own careful review and assessment of how well that plan was actually fulfilled in quantifiable terms.

If you can't measure it, you can't assume you achieved the goals or won the battle! This process of review and assessment must take place on a regular basis.

"Beware of the man who won't be bothered with details."

William Feather

The 90-Day Review

The suggested timeline for family-owned businesses is to carefully review and assess progress toward key strategic goals (targeted outcomes) once every ninety days. This is a standard that works well for businesses of all sizes. Yet many family-owned businesses begin life without much meaningful experience or many role models when it comes to "review and assessment." In that case, special effort is required.

Many startups, and particularly family-owned startups, are quite comfortable with a "seat of the pants" approach to planning, especially in the early days of the business. The closeness of some family members, the sense of committed partnership they share, their knowledge of each other's goals, and their ability to cover for each other and compensate for each other's blind spots -- are all positives. However, these factors can sometimes make the lack of a formal planning process seem natural, like an integral part of "how we do business around here."

Yet if the plan is to GROW the business, then "how we do business" must change! It is impossible to overstate the importance of establishing and holding to a pattern of 90 day review and assessment, regardless of the size of your business. If you make the mistake of "planning" three to five years at a time, and then "reviewing" your results only periodically, you will not be able to support a pattern of intelligent, planned growth for your business. What are your targeted outcomes?

Targeted Outcomes				
Revenues	100X	200X	300X	400X
Profits	10X	20X	30X	40X
Orders	20	40	60	80
Days	90	180	270	360

Build the Team

Strategic Benchmarking

If you create a written plan that all your team members have input on and know about, and if you measure the deliverables connected to that plan in a consistent way that everyone on the team can see and understand, an amazing thing happens. You will find the entire team -- G1, G2, G3 and everyone else -- getting behind your plan. That means they are more likely to be committed to achieving or overachieving on the results!

In effect, that's what all the benchmarking tools (Key Performance Indicators – KPIs) really are: team-building tools. All the metrics, all the flash reports (dashboards), all the daily call reports are there for one reason: to improve the team and its efforts. Your goal is to get everyone in the organization using these tools to identify, compare and measure themselves against the correct metrics, so that everyone, not just management, is comparing the targeted outcomes in the plan against the real-world results delivered.

By the way, this may be the single best way to relieve financial-based tensions in the family-owned business. Set clear benchmarks and clear rewards for hitting key benchmarks so that all employees are "playing by the same set of rules."

Everyone in your family-owned business should have a clear picture of what his or her measurable personal goals are for the quarter, their personal and team benchmarks relevant to that goal and how their personal contributions are, day by day, either moving the company closer to, or standing in the way of, fulfilling that goal.

It is impossible to implement a vigorous growth plan for your family-owned business without a sense of communal buy-in! That's why using benchmarks in this team focused manner is such a critical step. Clear benchmarks are what give the team's undertakings a sense of fairness, a shared vocabulary and a feeling of group cohesion. Everyone is in it together, and everyone is in it to win it.

Flash Report (Dashboard) Metrics – Key Performance Indicators (KPIs)				
Quotes	Sales	Production	Shipped	Payroll
50	100X	20	15	25X
100	200X	40	45	50X
150	300X	60	55	75X
200	400X	80	85	100X

It all begins with setting the strategy and identifying the right performance targets that connect to that strategy. Get input on how your company's strategic goals (targeted outcomes) connect to the activity of the individual teams; get consensus on the goals; communicate the strategy up and down your family-owned business so you can create some "buzz" around exactly what's happening next, when it's happening and what the rewards will be.

You can do this easily by taking a three-tiered "breakeven – good – stretch" approach to identifying the most important strategic goals. So for instance, if your sales team as a whole has the goal of bringing in a total of thirty new accounts this quarter, break that down into measurable goals for each individual member of the team. What is each team member's personal "break even" goal going to be in terms of closed sales 90 days from now? What about a "good" level goal for 90 days from now? What is the "stretch" level of performance?

Work with the sales team to come up with a series of individual "good" performance goals that add up to the thirty new accounts for the company as a whole. Track each salesperson's progress toward that "good" goal in a visual way that everyone in the department can see, and also track metrics (such as voice-to-voice discussions with brand new sales leads) that support the goal.

Focusing on the metrics in this way makes everyone more effective, and allows you to move past all the "clutter" and focus on exactly what needs to happen next to support your growth plans. You will know that you have implemented the advice shared here when you notice fewer and more productive meetings. If you don't see that happening, you haven't yet focused effectively on the benchmarks! Typically, you will see a 25% and 30% improvement in meeting efficiency and time allocation.

	Targeted Outcomes			
	Phone	Visit	Quotes	New Accounts
Stretch				
Good				
Breakeven				
Days	90	180	270	360

Support Your Strategic Goals

It is extremely important to call in the aid of the professionals already working for your business -- accountants, bankers, lawyers and so forth -- in support of the implementation of your company's plan. You should do this in assessing both the short-term and long-term plans you have put together. Perhaps the simplest and most effective way to do this is to take your banker out to lunch once a quarter -- and pay for lunch. During that meeting, discuss all the various aspects of your strategic plan!

Accountants, bankers, lawyers and other professional advisors typically have deep experience; they have lots of insights that can help your growing business. These professionals are particularly important in a family business, where they represent an important buffer for dealing with G1 and G2 issues, and can help to resolve many conflicts. And if your family-owned business is not yet in the 90-day assessment "rhythm," these people will help you get there.

Summary

Anything worth doing well in support of your growth plan is worth measuring. You must confirm that what's happening today is being executed well and is actually contributing to the growth of your business. Whether you have done so in the past or not, get into a habit of reviewing measurable progress toward your goal every 90 days. After all, anything worth measuring today is worth measuring again 90 days from now!

When looking at financial goals and other quantifiable targets, work collaboratively to identify exactly what constitutes:

▶ Breakeven performance

▶ Good performance

▶ Stretch performance

Then build your family business around a quarterly review that tells you whether you have attained or exceeded those strategic benchmarks!

"A wise man will make more opportunities than he finds."

Francis Bacon

tip 10

Celebration
Pop the Cork

As a general but reliable rule, most family-owned businesses don't find enough reasons to celebrate in the workplace. STRATEGIC CELEBRATION can be a critical growth engine for your family's company. Don't overlook it!

It is important that your company find new and energizing ways to celebrate personal and organizational victories, be they large or small. Yet many family-owned businesses overlook this step. Sometimes, this is because there is simply not a strong tradition of celebrating victories and/or forward progress on the part of the founding (G1) generation of the business, and the successive generations that adapt the founder's personality or attitude toward celebrating.

Yet this is not a "personality issue." It is a strategic issue! If the "family tradition" at your company is to celebrate once a year and only once a year, such as during a holiday party, then it is time for that tradition to change. Celebration is an extremely important strategic tool, one that consistently separates high-growth family-owned businesses from ones that experience slow (or no) growth.

Here's the bottom line: If your people don't find reasons to celebrate what they do for a living, you shouldn't expect their families to celebrate what they do either! When your people go home after work do they share the joy of work with their families? This is the true measurement of celebration.

"The more you praise and celebrate life, the more there is in life to celebrate."

Oprah Winfrey

Celebration, in all its varied forms, ties us back to the organization's mission. It reinforces the powerful human experience of positive emotion on achieving a chosen personal and/or business goal.

It's not enough to gather people together once a year for an office party, or reward the silting for hitting the annual quota. Although those are both certainly good things to do, they are not evidence of a daily culture of celebrating.

The strategic goal must be to promote the act of celebration itself as part of "how we do things around here" so that some kind of celebration happens frequently for every single employee. If you think your team has "no time" to celebrate its accomplishments, or to appropriately acknowledge a team member who crosses a personal finish line as "distracting," you may be in for a surprise.

Give STRATEGIC CELEBRATION a try for just 90 days, and you will see just how much more productive celebration-focused teams can be!

As a bare minimum -- and only as a starting point -- ask yourself this question: Do we have a Star of the Month program in place? This program celebrates someone on your team who went "above and beyond the call" within the last thirty days and shares exactly HOW the person achieved an outcome that brought the company closer to fulfilling its mission. This is STRATEGIC CELEBRATION in a nutshell.

It is remarkable how many family-owned businesses do not celebrate their Star of the Month team members. If yours is one of them, change the pattern. Start this month! Begin celebrating the people who come up with new best practices and make sure everyone knows what they did right. By taking this one simple step, you can transform your entire business. *(Word of warning: Some employees, probably a minority, will be uncomfortable being acknowledged publicly. Find other ways to celebrate them and celebrate their contributions.)*

Celebration

Daily Activity

STRATEGIC CELEBRATION can and should happen *throughout* the day, and it can make all the difference in terms of workplace productivity. It can make teams dramatically more committed to the company mission and dramatically more efficient.

One good example of a culture of daily celebration that's been "hard-wired" into a family-owned business comes from a mid-western office furniture and workplace design firm in Chicago. The company hands out postcards to customers for them to use as vehicles for commenting about the service they received from one of the company's employees. Whenever anyone on the team gets a positive postcard, that person is encouraged to post it in his or her work area. The simple act of receiving a postcard is a cause for "instant celebration" -- positive acknowledgement among one's coworkers at multiple points during the day.

Parties are fine. There are plenty of successful companies out there that appoint someone on the team whose official responsibility is to find good reasons to have a party! But a party is not the only way to celebrate good results. A brief, informal one-on-one conversation acknowledging that someone has done a great job can be just as important to your family-owned business.

Party During Tough Times

The US economy is finally emerging from a sustained financial downturn, and we are finally seeing more celebrations and public acknowledgments of personal achievement in the workplace. This is of course a good thing, but the reality is that you need to celebrate forward progress even more when there are major challenges facing your family-owned company. A recession is when you need the celebration most!

When the obstacles are big, make sure you help your team to find a way to focus on the positive. One advertising agency decided to throw a party after the team lost a major account. Why? The owner of the agency wanted to celebrate three things: first that the team had figured out exactly what mistakes it had made to lose the account; second, that it would not repeat the mistakes; and third, that it was committed, both as a group and individually, to a significantly higher level of performance in the future. He was right on all three counts. That really was a great reason to celebrate!

You could also identify new ways to celebrate and reward positive open feedback from your associates. If the person's input made your workplace safer, more focused on quality, or better able to serve its customers, you should find some way to reward that associate -- particularly if it took courage to speak up!

Barry-Wehmiller, a global supplier of manufacturing technology and services strives to be the kind of company that people enjoy working for. It's what they mean at this 125 year old family-owned business when they say, "We measure success by the way we touch the lives of people." Despite economic downturns, Barry-Wehmiller is a well-balanced and financially solid company with a healthy pattern of continued growth.

Celebrate "Baby Steps"

It's important to find an appropriate way to celebrate the steps along the way that lead toward attaining a major goal that ties into your company's mission. Don't just reward the end result!

Celebrate the commitment to the goal. Celebrate the training that takes place, the practice, the learning moments, the personal commitments to improve, the personal and team milestones. Every "baby step" along the way can be a reason to celebrate, acknowledge and positively reinforce your team members.

As long as learning, measurable forward progress, or some combination of the two took place, you've got something to celebrate! The intermediate accomplishments you celebrate can be "baby steps" that make your employees happier, healthier or more productive during the work day. One company decided to emphasize fitness in the workforce, and held a contest that rewarded the employee who safely lost the highest number of pounds!

These kinds of celebrations may result in major positive life events for your associates, personal "high points" that connect to significantly greater productivity, team cohesiveness and personal and organizational achievement. Look for new opportunities to create these moments!

Whenever you make celebration a credible and consistent part of the workforce culture, you make everyone in the organization feel as though they're part of the family!

Pop the cork! Make STRATEGIC CELEBRATION "the way we do things around here." Initiate, support and reward a company culture that celebrates proof that the company, and/or any individual within it, is moving closer to fulfilling its mission. Celebrate the big steps toward attaining important goals. Celebrate the little steps. Celebrate everything in between!

Quite simply, do your associates celebrate at home the joy of being part of your team?

"You don't learn to walk by following rules. You learn by doing, and by falling over."

Richard Branson

About the Author

R. Craig Palubiak is the founder of Optim Consulting Group, a management consulting firm that specializes in facilitating business and growth strategies. His clients range from small privately owned to Fortune 500 companies.

Craig has been a business owner (two national firms) and a corporate executive with Enterprise Rent-A-Car where under his guidance commercial leasing became the first national division. He is a noted author, professional speaker and an adjunct professor.

optimgroupusa.com

cpalubiak@optimgroupusa.com

Notes

Made in the USA
Charleston, SC
11 March 2016